SPACE FLIGHT ADVENTURES AND DISASTERS

THE TRAGEDY OF THE SPACE SHUTTLE CHALLENGER

A MYREPORTLINKS.COM BOOK

HENRY M. HOLDEN

MyReportLinks.com Books
an imprint of

Enslow Publishers, Inc.
Box 398, 40 Industrial Road
Berkeley Heights, NJ 07922
USA

MyReportLinks.com Books, an imprint of Enslow Publishers, Inc. MyReportLinks® is a registered trademark of Enslow Publishers, Inc.

Library of Congress Cataloging-in-Publication Data

Holden, Henry M.
  The tragedy of the space shuttle Challenger / Henry M. Holden.
      p. cm. — (Space flight adventures and disasters)
Summary: Describes the events surrounding the explosion of the Challenger shuttle in 1986, the investigation of this disaster, and the seven astronauts who died. Includes Internet links to related Web sites, source documents, and photographs.
Includes bibliographical references and index.
  ISBN 0-7660-5165-X
  1. Challenger (Spacecraft)—Accidents—Juvenile literature. 2. Space shuttles—Accidents—Juvenile literature. [1. Challenger (Spacecraft)—Accidents. 2. Space shuttles—Accidents.] I. Title. II. Series.
  TL867.H65 2004
  363.12'465—dc22

                              2003014490

Printed in the United States of America

10 9 8 7 6 5 4 3 2 1

To Our Readers:
Through the purchase of this book, you and your library gain access to the Report Links that specifically back up this book.
The Publisher will provide access to the Report Links that back up this book and will keep these Report Links up to date on **www.myreportlinks.com** for three years from the book's first publication date.
We have done our best to make sure all Internet addresses in this book were active and appropriate when we went to press. However, the author and the Publisher have no control over, and assume no liability for, the material available on those Internet sites or on other Web sites they may link to.
The usage of the MyReportLinks.com Books Web site is subject to the terms and conditions stated on the Usage Policy Statement on **www.myreportlinks.com**.
A password may be required to access the Report Links that back up this book. The password is found on the bottom of page 4 of this book.
Any comments or suggestions can be sent by e-mail to comments@myreportlinks.com or to the address on the back cover.

Photo Credits: BBC News Online, p. 30; Challenger Center for Space Education, p. 37; *Life* magazine, p. 27; MyReportLinks.com Books, p. 4; National Aeronautics and Space Administration (NASA), pp. 3, 9, 10, 12, 15, 16, 18, 20, 22, 24, 25, 26, 33, 35, 41; Photos.com, p.1; The Astronauts Memorial Foundation, p. 39.

Cover Photo: NASA

Cover Description: The crew of the Space Shuttle *Challenger* flight STS 51-L.

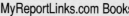
Contents

MyReportLinks.com Books
Great Books, Great Links, Great for Research!

The Report Links listed on the following four pages can save you hours of research time by **instantly** bringing you to the best Web sites relating to your report topic.

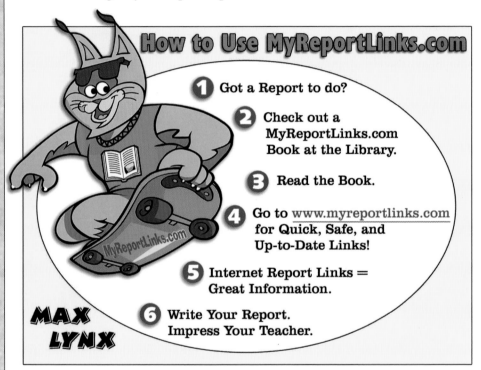

How to Use MyReportLinks.com

1. Got a Report to do?
2. Check out a MyReportLinks.com Book at the Library.
3. Read the Book.
4. Go to www.myreportlinks.com for Quick, Safe, and Up-to-Date Links!
5. Internet Report Links = Great Information.
6. Write Your Report. Impress Your Teacher.

MAX LYNX

The pre-evaluated Web sites are your links to source documents, photographs, illustrations, and maps. They also provide links to dozens—even hundreds—of Web sites about your report subject.

MyReportLinks.com Books and the MyReportLinks.com Web site save you time and make report writing easier than ever!

Please see "To Our Readers" on the copyright page for important information about this book, the MyReportLinks.com Web site, and the Report Links that back up this book. Please enter **FCH5511** if asked for a password.

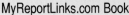
Report Links

 The Internet sites described below can be accessed at
http://www.myreportlinks.com

*EDITOR'S CHOICE

▶**The *Challenger* Disaster: Ten Years Later**
The *Life* magazine Web site holds a dedication to Christa McAuliffe
and the rest of the *Challenger* crew. Here you will find many images of
McAuliffe during her training. You will also learn how the *Challenger*
disaster affected space travel.

*EDITOR'S CHOICE

▶**The *Challenger* Legacy**
From the Spaceline Web site you can read an article discussing the
Challenger disaster. It includes the Rogers Commission reports,
and revisions made to the space shuttle launch policies as a result
of the accident.

*EDITOR'S CHOICE

▶**Space Shuttle *Challenger* 1986**
This Web site explores what happened to the *Challenger*. Here you will
learn about the O-rings and Solid Rocket Boosters, two components of
the space shuttle that failed.

*EDITOR'S CHOICE

▶**Kennedy Space Center**
At the Kennedy Space Center Web site you can explore the center's
history, learn about space shuttles, and obtain the latest news from
"NASA Direct."

*EDITOR'S CHOICE

▶**Biographical Data: S. Christa Corrigan McAuliffe**
From the Lyndon B. Johnson Space Center you will find the
biographical data on Christa McAuliffe. Learn about her education,
organizations she belonged to, her NASA experience, and other facts
about her life.

*EDITOR'S CHOICE

▶**Looking Back At the *Challenger* Disaster**
Learn about the *Challenger* disaster, and the investigation that followed,
from various articles posted here. This site also includes some articles
dealing with the explosion of the *Columbia* space shuttle.

Report Links

The Internet sites described below can be accessed at http://www.myreportlinks.com

▷**Address to the Nation on the *Challenger* Disaster**

Read the speech that Ronald Reagan gave to the nation shortly after the *Challenger* disaster.

▷**The Astronauts Memorial Foundation**

At the Astronauts Memorial Foundation you can visit the memorial honoring astronauts who gave their lives for the space program.

▷**Biographical Data: Ellison S. Onizuka**

At the Lyndon B. Johnson Space Center Web site you will find the biographical data on Ellison S. Onizuka. Here you will learn about his education, organizations he belonged to, his NASA experience, and other facts about his life.

▷**Biographical Data: Francis R. "Dick" Scobee**

The Lyndon B. Johnson Space Center contains biographical data on Francis R. "Dick" Scobee. It covers his education, organizations he belonged to, his NASA experience, and other facts about his life.

▷**Biographical Data: Gregory B. Jarvis**

The Lyndon B. Johnson Space Center contains biographical data on Gregory B. Jarvis. Learn about his education, organizations he belonged to, his NASA experience, and other facts about his life.

▷**Biographical Data: Judith A. Resnik**

The Lyndon B. Johnson Space Center houses the biographical data on Judith A. Resnik. Her education, organizations she belonged to, and details of her NASA experience are just some of the facts presented.

▷**Biographical Data: Michael J. Smith**

Biographical data about Michael J. Smith.

▷**Biographical Data: Ronald E. McNair**

Biographical data covering the life of Ronald E. McNair.

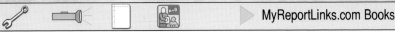
The Internet sites described below can be accessed at
http://www.myreportlinks.com

▶*Challenger* **Center for Space Science Education**

The *Challenger* Center for Space Science Education was created by the families who lost loved ones in the *Challenger* disaster. At this Web site you will learn about the center's activities and efforts.

▶**The *Challenger* Disaster**

This Web site presents a discussion of what went wrong during the *Challenger* launch. Topics include profiles of the key players, the Rogers Commission, and ethical issues related to the disaster.

▶*Challenger* **Time Line**

At the Spaceflight Now Web site you can view a time line of the *Challenger* take off. You will also find several video clips of the mission.

▶**51-L The *Challenger* Accident**

Many articles and links to Web sites related to the *Challenger* disaster can be accessed here. Topics include causes, safety, the Rogers Commission report, and many other issues.

▶**NASA**

The National Aeronautics and Space Administration Web site has information about all things related to space travel and exploration. Click on "Missions" to learn about future and historical missions.

▶**NASA: History Office**

At the NASA History Office Web site you can explore scientific and technological accomplishments.

▶**NASA Human Space Flight**

The NASA Human Space Flight Web site can teach you about space stations and space shuttles. Learn about missions, and find out what happens behind the scenes. You can also get the latest "Space News."

▶**NASA Kids**

The NASA Kids Web site has sections called "Rockets and Airplanes," "Earth," "Astronauts Living in Space," "Space and Beyond," and discusses many other interesting topics.

Report Links

The Internet sites described below can be accessed at http://www.myreportlinks.com

▶**NASA Quest**

The NASA Quest Web site gives visitors an opportunity to explore and learn about NASA. Here you can read the biographies of NASA employees and learn about aerospace technology and space exploration events.

▶**1986: Seven Dead in Space Shuttle Disaster**

From this BBC News Web site you will find an article about the *Challenger* disaster. There is also a clickable time line of space travel events. Each event is linked to an article.

▶**On This Day**

From The *New York Times* Learning Network you can read an article about the *Challenger* disaster. This article focuses on Christa McAuliffe, the high school teacher who was the winner of the nationwide contest for the first teacher to go to space.

▶**Sally Ride**

The National Women's History Museum Web site has a profile of Sally Ride, the first American woman to go to space. Ride was chosen to help investigate what happened to the *Challenger*.

▶**Shuttles and Space Stations**

At *The World Almanac for Kids Online* Web site you can view a space travel time line of events that took place from 1977 to 2001. Here you will find links to profiles of Sally Ride and John Glenn. Click on "Space Shuttle" to learn about the *Challenger* disaster.

▶**Space Shuttle *Challenger* Memorial**

The Space Shuttle *Challenger* Memorial is located at Arlington National Cemetery. The cemetery's Web site lets you view the monument and read the dedication.

▶**"They Slipped the Surly Bonds of Earth to Touch the Face of God"**

This *Time* magazine article recounts the events leading up to the *Challenger* launch and the country's reaction after the explosion.

▶**The White House and Space Exploration**

The White House Historical Society Web site provides information about monumental moments in space travel and exploration history, including the *Challenger* disaster.

Fateful Mission	51-L, January 28, 1986
Total Missions of Orbiter	10 missions, 69 days in space
Manufacturer	Rockwell
Astronauts	• Francis R. Scobee, *Commander* • Michael J. Smith, *Pilot* • Judith A. Resnik, *Mission Specialist 1* • Ellison S. Onizuka, *Mission Specialist 2* • Ronald E. McNair, *Mission Specialist 3* • Gregory B. Jarvis, *Payload Specialist 1* • Sharon Christa McAuliffe, *Payload Specialist 2* from Teacher In Space Program
Memorial	On May 20, 1986, a memorial featuring the faces of the crew members was placed at Arlington National Cemetery to honor the astronauts.

The Challenger *flight 51–L* ▶
mission patch.

THE FINAL VOYAGE

It was early Tuesday morning, January 28, 1986. The weather at Cape Canaveral was frigid. The night before, the temperature had gone below freezing. People could plainly see icicles on the launchpad. The Florida sun was warming the air and would soon begin to melt the two-foot icicles. It was the coldest day ever for a space shuttle launch.

This launch had captured worldwide attention. It was going to carry Sharon Christa McAuliffe, a history teacher,

▲ On the morning of January 28, 1986, icicles covered the launchpad at Cape Canaveral.

into space.[1] She was going to be the first passenger/observer of the Teacher in Space Program.

There were concerns in the Mission Control Center. They had asked for three ice inspections of the rockets and the shuttle *Challenger*. The third inspection, shortly before launch, showed the ice had melted onto the launchpad.

The flight had been postponed six times due to bad weather and mechanical issues. There had been another two-hour delay earlier in the morning. A part in the launch processing system had failed during fueling.

At T-(for takeoff) minus six seconds, *Challenger*'s main engines fired. Huge billowing columns of flame and smoke surrounded the base of the shuttle. Within four seconds, the engines were burning at 90 percent power.

The launch is the most dangerous part of the flight. The external fuel tank was filled with 528,600 gallons (over 2 million liters) of explosive fuel. They help generate 2.6 million pounds (1.7 million kilograms) of thrust.

At T-minus zero seconds, the two white solid fuel rocket boosters ignited. These were attached to each side of the huge external fuel tank. Each of the boosters carried more than 1.1 million pounds (498,952 kilograms) of solid fuel. They were to help the main engines lift the shuttle to a speed of 3,512 miles per hour (5,652 kilometers per hour). The shuttle roared off the pad and into the sky. Five miles (8 kilograms) away, hundreds of spectators could feel the ground shaking beneath them.[2]

Liftoff

Liftoff occurred at 11:38 A.M. The rockets boosted the shuttle off the launchpad. *Challenger* arched up through the air, leaving a thick trail of smoke behind. This was *Challenger*'s tenth mission. Christa McAuliffe and the crew, commander

△ *Millions watched in horror as white trails of smoke lay in the sky where the* Challenger *had once been.*

Francis "Dick" Scobee, pilot Michael J. Smith, and mission specialists Judith A. Resnik, Ellison S. Onizuka, Ronald E. McNair, and Gregory B. Jarvis, awaited the upcoming mission.

For the first sixty seconds, all systems seemed to work perfectly. At T+plus seventy seconds, Mission Control told Commander Scobee to "throttle up." This means the pilot increases the speed of the shuttle. Three seconds later, Smith said, "uhh . . . oh!"[3] Then all communications ended.[4]

Millions of people were watching on television. Due to the fact that Christa McAullife was on board, thousands of schoolchildren were part of this audience. They were following the thick white vapor trail behind the shuttle. At 58.8 seconds into the flight, a flame, later seen on enhanced film, was coming from the right solid rocket booster. At 72 seconds, there was a sudden chain of events that destroyed *Challenger* and the seven crew members on board. All of these events happened in less than two seconds. A huge white cloud formed where the shuttle had been. From within the white cloud came a horrific flaming ball of fire.

Moments before, people had been filled with joy. Now no one could believe what he or she had just seen. The rocket had blown to pieces. It was the worst tragedy in the history of the space program. Perhaps not until the attack on the World Trade Center towers, on September 11, 2001, did American children and adults have such a terrible feeling inside, as they did when they watched the destruction of *Challenger*. Sadly, this would not be the last time the world would watch a space shuttle tragedy. On February 1, 2003, the shuttle *Columbia* broke apart on reentry into Earth's atmosphere.

LAUNCH BACKGROUND

Challenger was the name of the orbiter that was to carry the astronauts into space. It was attached to a large orange external fuel tank and two solid rocket boosters. It was the second shuttle built, and it had joined the National Aeronautics and Space Administration (NASA) fleet in 1982. It was named for a ship that explored uncharted ocean waters a century earlier.

▶ **Launch Delays**

Challenger STS (flight) 51–L was scheduled to launch in July 1985. However, by the time the crew was assigned, the launch had been postponed to November. The *Challenger* launch was now far behind schedule. *Challenger* was finally rescheduled for launch in late January. The pressure was on NASA. Additional delays would have a negative effect on the coming shuttle launches. They, too, would have to be postponed.

On Monday, January 27, the Florida temperatures began to drop. At night, they dipped to 24°F (−4°C) at the launch site. The wind chill factor made it feel as if it was ten degrees below zero (−23°C).[1] At dawn, the temperature began slowly rising. Engineers from the company that built the solid fuel rocket boosters were worried. They had experience with launches in cold weather. It could be dangerous to the astronauts. On earlier flights, some rubber seals, called O-rings, within the solid rocket boosters suffered damage from superheated gases.

Astronaut Bio: Christa McAuliffe 3/87 - Microsoft Internet Explorer

File Edit View Favorites Tools Help

Address http://www.jsc.nasa.gov/Bios/htmlbios/mcauliffe.html   Go Links

Biographical Data

Lyndon B. Johnson Space Center
Houston, Texas 77058

NASA
National Aeronautics and
Space Administration

S. CHRISTA CORRIGAN MCAULIFFE
TEACHER IN SPACE PARTICIPANT (DECEASED)

PERSONAL DATA: Born September 2, 1948 in Boston, Massachusetts. She is survived by husband Steven and two children. Her listed recreational interests included jogging, tennis, and volleyball.

EDUCATION: Graduated from Marian High School, Framingham, Massachusetts, in 1966; received a bachelor of arts degree, Framingham State College, 1970; and a masters degree in education, Bowie State College, Bowie, Maryland, 1978.

ORGANIZATIONS: Board member, New Hampshire Council of Social Studies; National Council of Social Studies; Concord Teachers Association; New Hampshire Education Association; and the National Education Association.

OUTSIDE ACTIVITIES: Member, Junior Service League; teacher, Christian Doctrine Classes, St. Peters Church; host family, A Better Chance Program (ABC), for inner-city students; and fundraiser for

http://www.jsc.nasa.gov/Bios/   Internet

⊿ *Christa McAuliffe was going to teach two lessons aboard the shuttle. The first was about the crew, cockpit, and eating and exercising in a weightless environment. The second was to explain how the shuttle flew, and the purpose of space exploration.*

The damage had occurred at launch temperatures much higher than on this day. Up to that time, the lowest launch temperature had been 53°F (11.7°C). However, because the engineers could not show positive proof the launch could be dangerous, NASA decided to launch *Challenger* anyway.

The NASA television cameras showed the astronauts shivering in the icy wind. They walked carefully along the giant steel-framed gantry, two hundred feet above the launchpad. They did not want to slip and fall on the ice.[2]

As the sun rose, it revealed a clear blue, cloudless sky. It looked like a perfect day to fly. However, it was still too cold. It was about 28°F (−2.2°C), and there was ice on the launchpad.[3] At T-minus nine minutes, there was a routine ten-minute hold. NASA would extend this hold until the temperature rose to 36°F (2.2°C).[4]

By 11:00 A.M., almost four hours later, the sun had warmed the outside of the launch vehicle. Everyone expected the countdown to resume shortly. Twenty minutes before liftoff, the "ice team" made another inspection. An engineer watching on closed-circuit television from California called the Cape. He asked them to delay the launch.[5] The warm sun on the outside would not solve the problem that worried him. Without the direct rays of the sun, the rubber O-rings would stay cold and brittle. The more brittle the O-rings, the greater the chance they would fail.

▲ At 11:38 A.M. on the morning of January 28, 1986, Challenger lifted off the ground.

NASA resumed the countdown, and *Challenger* lifted off. It was the twenty-fifth shuttle mission in less than five years. Many thought the flights were now routine and that all the danger had been eliminated.

Rocket Ignition

When the solid rocket boosters fired, a puff of black smoke came from the lower joint of the right booster rocket. At the time, no one noticed the black smoke because it mixed in with the regular ignition smoke. Almost as quickly as it appeared, it was gone.

Any engine failure during launch would call for a "RTLS"—Return To Launch Site.[6] The pilot could fire bolts that would release the orbiter from the fuel tank and boosters.[7] *Challenger* would then land at the Kennedy Space Center or another landing spot. The earliest point this could happen is after the solid rocket boosters had burned out and dropped off. This would be about two and a half minutes into the launch.[8] The shuttle cannot physically separate while the solid rocket boosters are thrusting.[9] As a result, there would be no escape for the *Challenger* astronauts. On this launch, there was no warning of a malfunction. Seventy-three seconds into the launch, *Challenger* exploded. It had been traveling at almost twice the speed of sound when the explosion tore it to pieces.[10] It did not look like anyone could have survived the horrific blast. The crew cabin, forming the nose of *Challenger*, survived the blast intact. For a few moments, it continued upward, to an altitude of 65,000 feet (19,812 meters).[11] It then fell toward the ocean below. The disaster was the worst for NASA since the first *Apollo* moon capsule burned on its launchpad in 1967, killing three astronauts.

▲ *Christa McAuliffe's sister (left) and parents console each other after the* Challenger *explosion.*

▷ Shock and Disbelief

The accident became one of the most significant events of the 1980s. Millions around the world watched it on live television. A moment earlier, the students at Christa McAuliffe's Concord, New Hampshire, high school were cheering the launch. Her parents, Ed and Grace Corrigan, had flown to the Cape with eighteen third graders to watch the launch.[12] They all stared in disbelief. McAuliffe's husband, Steven, her son, Scott, and daughter, Caroline, sat in McAuliffe's dormitory room in shock. Jane Smith, wife of pilot Mike Smith, knew something terrible had happened. "They're gone," she said. Her son asked, "What do you mean, Mom?" "They're lost," was all

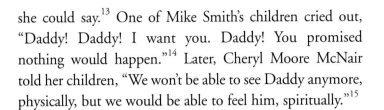

she could say.[13] One of Mike Smith's children cried out, "Daddy! Daddy! I want you. Daddy! You promised nothing would happen."[14] Later, Cheryl Moore McNair told her children, "We won't be able to see Daddy anymore, physically, but we would be able to feel him, spiritually."[15]

For thirty seconds, the loudspeakers at the launch site were silent. By then everyone realized the cloud of smoke from the rockets was no longer rising. Then, over the loudspeakers, came a voice from Mission Control. "Flight controllers are looking very carefully at the situation. Obviously a major malfunction. We have no downlink." This meant there were no data or radio signals coming from the shuttle. Then, what many had suspected was confirmed. "We have a report . . . that the vehicle has exploded."[16]

Immediately after the explosion, the astronaut's families were put in buses and rushed to the crew's quarters. NASA wanted to get them away from the reporters. There would be too many questions and no answers, yet.

▶ Crew Recovery

It took about an hour for the debris to stop raining down from the sky. Then, NASA began a search-and-rescue effort for survivors although no one really believed anyone could have survived the explosion. Late that afternoon, NASA announced there were no signs that the crew had survived.

In Washington, D.C., President Ronald Reagan was going to give his State of the Union speech that evening. When he heard about the accident, he canceled his speech. Instead, he used the time to talk to the nation. "The future does not belong to the fainthearted; it belongs to the brave," he said. "The *Challenger* crew was

pulling us into the future, and we'll continue to follow them."[17]

Dozens of ships and aircraft searched for debris. The search covered about 1,200 square miles (3,108 square kilometers) of ocean. The ships used electronic devices such as sonar to look for pieces of wreckage. Mini-submarines searched for the astronauts. Some of the wreckage was over 1,000 feet (304.8 meters) down. All floating debris and any underwater debris considered important would be collected and brought ashore.

On March 9, recovery teams found the crew cabin in 100 feet (30.5 meters) of water. The bodies of the astronauts were inside, still strapped in their seats. Scientists studied the wreckage in an attempt to determine what

▲ This portion of Challenger's right wing was recovered seventy nautical miles northeast of Cape Canaveral by Navy divers.

killed the crew. The crew compartment was hardened and found separate from the shuttle cargo bay. However, the crash of the crew compartment into the ocean was violent. The force of the impact was far more than the human body could withstand.[18]

NASA could not positively determine what had killed the astronauts. It was possible they said, but not certain, that the crew lost consciousness in the seconds following the explosion. At an altitude of 45,000 feet (13,716 meters), when the explosion took place, loss of cabin pressure would have caused rapid loss of consciousness. The explosion stopped the flow of oxygen to the crew. Each crew member had a personal air pack with an emergency oxygen supply. These must be turned on by hand. Searchers found four air packs. Three of them had been turned on.[19] More than half the air in these packs had been used. Some of the crew may have lived long enough to activate their emergency air supplies. It took about two–and–a–half minutes for the crew compartment to fall to the ocean. It fell at about 200 miles per hour (321.9 kilometers per hour). The impact with the ocean had probably caused their deaths. By then, all of the crew members were most likely unconscious.[20]

Chapter 3 ▶

THE SEVEN HEROES

There are three types of astronauts on a typical shuttle flight: the flight crew, mission specialists, and payload specialists. They each have specific jobs.

The *Challenger* crew was an example of diversity at its best. They mirrored the American population in terms of race, gender, and religion. Among the seven heroes was an African American, Caucasian Americans, and an Asian American. There were women, Christians, a Jew, and a Buddhist.

▲ The seven crew members represented a diverse American population. From left to right: (top row) Ellison Onizuka, Christa McAuliffe, Gregory B. Javis, Judith A. Resnik, (bottom row) Michael J. Smith, Dick Scobee, Ronald E. McNair.

▶ Flight Crew

The flight crew consists of the shuttle commander and the pilot. The commander is in charge of the shuttle and the crew and is responsible for the mission's success and safety. Forty-six-year-old spacecraft Commander Francis R. Scobee was a former Air Force mechanic. He had gone to night school and earned a college degree in engineering. This qualified him to become an officer and a pilot. He served in the Vietnam War and later became an Air Force test pilot. Scobee flew more than forty-five types of aircraft, logging more than 6,500 hours of flight time. He and his wife, June, had two children.

Scobee was the pilot on the fifth flight of *Challenger* in April 1984. During this mission, the crew successfully repaired a broken satellite. This was a very important mission. It showed that a shuttle crew could repair satellites in orbit. Scobee loved his job. He once said, "You know, it's a real crime to be paid for a job that I have so much fun doing."[1]

The pilot for mission 51–L was forty-year-old Captain Michael J. Smith. He was married to Jane Jarrell, and they had three children. Smith flew A–6 Intruders during the Vietnam War. Later he worked as a test pilot for the Navy, flying twenty-eight different aircraft. This was his first spaceflight.

▶ Mission Specialists

Mission specialists operate the mechanical systems on the shuttle. They may launch satellites and sometimes make spacewalks. Ellison S. Onizuka was thirty-nine years old and a lieutenant colonel in the Air Force. He and his wife, Lorna, had two children. He was born in Hawaii,

◄ *Judy Resnik was the second American woman in space. The thirty-six-year-old had an optimistic attitude and little fear of danger.*

to parents of Japanese-American descent. Before becoming an astronaut, he was a U.S. Air Force test pilot. He was the first Asian American in space when he climbed aboard the *Discovery* in 1985. This *Challenger* mission was his second spaceflight.

Thirty-six-year-old Judith A. Resnik had a doctorate degree in electrical engineering. She enjoyed playing classical piano. Resnik joined NASA with the first group of woman astronauts in 1978. In 1983, Sally Ride became the first American woman in space on board *Challenger*. Resnik became the second woman in space on board *Discovery* a year later. The dangers of space-flight did not worry Resnik. "I think something is only dangerous if you are not prepared for it," she said, "or if you don't have control over it or if you can't think through how to get yourself out of a problem."[2]

Ronald E. McNair was thirty-five years old and married to an educator, Cheryl Moore McNair. They had two children. McNair, born in South Carolina, attended the segregated public schools of the day. He studied hard and was the valedictorian of his high school class. He went on to attend Massachusetts Institute of Technology, where he specialized in laser physics and earned a doctorate degree.

Ronald E. McNair had flown on the Challenger *in 1984, becoming the second African American in space.*

McNair once told a group of students, "The true courage of spaceflight is not sitting aboard 6 million pounds of fire and thunder as one rockets away from this planet. True courage comes in enduring . . . and believing in oneself."[3] McNair became the second African American in space when he flew aboard the *Challenger* in 1984. During that mission, he operated the robotic arm used to move payloads in space.

Payload Specialists

Payload specialists are astronauts who carry out experiments on a flight. Perhaps the most excited crew member on *Challenger* was forty-one-year-old Gregory B. Jarvis. He had been scheduled for two earlier flights. He lost his place both times to members of Congress. Jarvis was married to Marcia Jarboe. He worked for the Hughes Aircraft Company and had a masters degree in electrical engineering. He had won his spot after competing against six hundred other employees. His main duty on *Challenger* would be to study liquids in microgravity. Like the other astronauts, Jarvis was not afraid of the dangers of

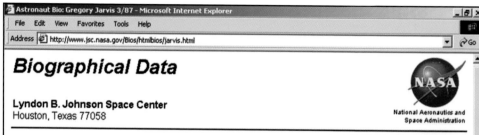

Biographical Data

Lyndon B. Johnson Space Center
Houston, Texas 77058

National Aeronautics and
Space Administration

NAME: Gregory B. Jarvis (Mr.)
Payload Specialist (Deceased)

PERSONAL DATA: Born August 24, 1944, in Detroit, Michigan. He is survived by his wife, Marcia. Greg Jarvis was an avid squash player and bicycle rider. He also enjoyed cross country skiing, backpacking, racquet ball, and white water river rafting. For relaxation, he played the classical guitar.

EDUCATION: Graduated from Mohawk Central High School, Mohawk, New York, 1962; received a bachelor of science degree in electrical engineering, State University of New York at Buffalo, 1967; a master's degree in electrical engineering, Northeastern University, Boston, Massachusetts, 1969. Mr. Jarvis also completed all of the course work for a master's degree in management science, West Coast University, Los Angeles, California.

EXPERIENCE: While pursuing his master's degree at Northeastern, Mr. Jarvis worked at Raytheon in Bedford Massachusetts, where he was involved in circuit design on the SAM-D missile. In July 1969, he entered active duty in the Air Force and was assigned to the Space Division in El Segundo, California. As a Communications Payload Engineer, in

---

Astronaut Gregory B. Jarvis received a master's degree in electrical engineering from Northeastern University in 1969—the same year he joined the Air Force. In 1984, he became payload specialist for NASA and was later chosen as a Challenger crew member.

spaceflight. "For any contingency, they know what to do," he said. "So I feel very, very comfortable. I'm excited, but not nervous."[4]

Thirty-six-year-old Sharon Christa McAuliffe taught in a New Hampshire high school. Her husband, Steven, was her high school sweetheart.[5] They had two children. McAuliffe liked classical music but preferred the Beatles.[6] She won her spot on the crew over thousands of teacher applicants. As a young girl, she was excited over the *Apollo* moon landings. When she was seven, she had asked why a monkey had gone into space instead of her.[7]

In 1984, McAuliffe learned about NASA's efforts to find "one of America's finest: a teacher."[8] She and the other applicants underwent tough physical and psychological tests similar to those given to astronauts. In July, McAuliffe was selected to be the first teacher in space.

She wrote on her astronaut application that, "I watched the Space Age being born and I would like to participate."[9] Now she would get her chance. McAuliffe had two jobs to do. The first was to demonstrate and explain to the children the effects of microgravity (free fall in orbit). She would do this via television from the shuttle.[10] The second was to videotape six science experiments.

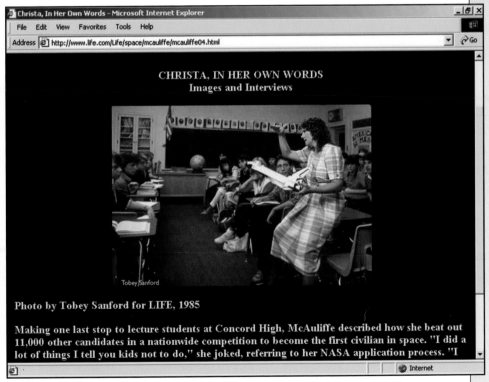

Christa, In Her Own Words - Microsoft Internet Explorer

File   Edit   View   Favorites   Tools   Help

Address http://www.life.com/Life/space/mcauliffe/mcauliffe04.html   Go

CHRISTA, IN HER OWN WORDS
Images and Interviews

Tobey Sanford

Photo by Tobey Sanford for LIFE, 1985

Making one last stop to lecture students at Concord High, McAuliffe described how she beat out 11,000 other candidates in a nationwide competition to become the first civilian in space. "I did a lot of things I tell you kids not to do," she joked, referring to her NASA application process. "I

Internet

▲ Christa McAuliffe's enthusiasm and determination were an inspiration to all. Before her mission she spoke to some of her students at Concord High School in New Hampshire. She explained how she was chosen and reminded them that anything is possible.

NASA would distribute these to schools around the country after the flight.[11]

McAuliffe was popular with the media, and the Teacher in Space Program earned positive publicity. Dick Scobee, the mission commander, told her, "You know, shuttle missions are taken for granted these days," he said, "but this one is unique. No matter what happens, this mission will always be remembered as the teacher-in-space mission, and you should be proud of that. We're all proud of that."[12] The death of McAuliffe and the crew forced NASA to reacknowledge the dangers of spaceflight and make safety changes.

President Reagan said after the accident, "We remember Christa McAuliffe, who captured the imagination of the entire nation, inspiring us with her pluck, her restless spirit of discovery; a teacher, not just to her students, but to an entire people, instilling us all with the excitement of this journey we ride into the future."[13]

The country was saddened by the accident. People wanted to know why seven brave, young, and intelligent men and women had died. They wanted those answers quickly.

Chapter 4

ANATOMY OF THE ACCIDENT

President Ronald Reagan appointed a special commission to find the cause of the accident. Among its members were General Charles Yeager, the first pilot to break the sound barrier, and Professor Neil Armstrong, the first person to walk on the moon. Dr. Sally Ride stopped training for what would have been her third spaceflight to join the commission.

Presidential Commission on the *Challenger* Accident

The commission became known as the Rogers Commission named after its chairperson, William P. Rogers. A former U.S. Attorney General and Secretary of State, Rogers was known for his fairness. The Rogers Commission was to investigate every phase of the doomed mission and find the cause of the explosion. It would also make recommendations to prevent it from happening again. However, any findings made would have to be backed up with physical proof. This meant examining the debris recovered from the ocean.

Recovery crews had brought up tons of wreckage. The larger pieces included parts of the shuttle and the external fuel tank. They recovered about half of the total vehicle, including both solid rocket boosters.[1] The wreckage was taken to a hangar at Cape Canaveral. There it was laid out on a grid and fitted back together wherever possible.

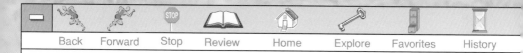

Divers also found the flight recorders. Clues as to what went wrong were found on these recorders.

▷ Important Clues

One important clue was a hole burned in part of the right solid rocket booster. While the investigators continued to look at the wreckage, the videotapes of the launch revealed solid clues. The team examined every frame of film and every frame of videotape. They found that less than half a second after ignition, there were puffs of black smoke coming from a joint on the right solid rocket booster. As the rocket rose, it left behind puffs of smoke. A fresh puff

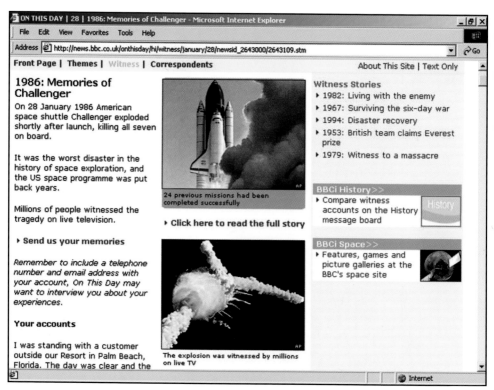

Milliseconds after ignition of the rocket carrying the space shuttle Challenger, puffs of black smoke were seen coming from the aft (or bottom). This was the first indication that something was not secured properly.

could then be seen near the joint.[2] Eight puffs of smoke appeared within two seconds. The smoke hinted there might be a tiny gap between two sections of the booster.

Something was burning that should not have been burning. The two boosters each are made of eleven cylinders, with walls about one-quarter-inch (.64 centimeters) thick. Tongue-and-groove joints and steel pins connect them to each other. Heat-resistant putty and a pair of synthetic rubber O-rings seal the joints. The O-ring's purpose is to seal the joints and prevent hot gases from escaping.[3]

The black color of the smoke suggested that the rubber O-rings were being burned away by the rocket's normal exhaust gases. The tape showed the smoke spreading across the booster, and then it was gone. No one saw this smoke during the launch. The commission looked at films of earlier launches to see if this smoke was present. It was not.

For almost a minute, the liftoff seemed normal. Then, from the flight recorder and the videotape, a terrible picture began to emerge. At 58.7 seconds, the smoke appeared again. At fifty-nine seconds, the greatest aerodynamic stress is on the vehicle. A second later, hot gas can be seen leaking from the right booster. A seal had burned away. The flight computer tried to adjust, to make up for the dropping fuel pressure in the booster. Seconds later, the computers show there was a problem in the liquid oxygen line. The tape showed that where the puffs of smoke had been, they had been replaced by a small flame. The flame had burned through the thin skin of the booster. It acted like a torch, burning through the bracket holding the external tank. The flame caused the bracket attached to the booster to break away. The booster then slammed into the external tank. This tank had a super explosive mixture of

fuel. At seventy-three seconds, there is a flash on the videotape, followed by the sound of an explosion on the flight recorder. Then all sounds and data stop.

An Accident Waiting to Happen

This was an accident, but one that did not have to happen. An engineer at Morton Thiokol, the company that made the rocket boosters, had said, ". . . if we do not take immediate action to dedicate a team to solve the problem, . . . then we stand in jeopardy of losing a flight . . . (and) a catastrophe of the highest order—loss of human life."[4] His words were ignored. He knew that someday an accident could occur.

NASA had known for years that the O-ring seals could fail. Out of the first twenty-four shuttle flights, inspections found fifteen instances where the O-rings had been partially burned away.[5] When NASA began using a new putty seal, the trouble got worse. There was damage to O-rings in eight of nine flights in 1985.[6] NASA never told the astronauts of the danger they faced.

Findings

The commission found both mechanical and human failures caused the accident. They concluded that the failure of an O-ring seal on the right solid rocket booster was the main cause of the explosion. However, why did the O-ring fail? The O-rings had frozen overnight, and at launch, the temperature of the left solid rocket booster was 33°F (.6°C). The right booster was 19°F (−7.2°C). The lower temperature was caused by the wind blowing off the super-cold external fuel tank.[7] In such cold, the rubber O-rings become stiff and inflexible. This allowed the rocket's hot gas to blow past the seal. A giant,

During Congressional hearings on the Challenger disaster, John W. Thomas, a NASA official, presents a duplicate of Challenger's O-ring seal to the House Science and Technology Committee.

nine–hundred–dollar rubber band was responsible for the loss of seven lives.

Morton Thiokol's engineers had been aware of the seal issue. Five months before the accident, they had submitted several design changes to NASA. These changes were expensive. NASA decided to delay the changes until the following year, when they had money in the budget.[8]

The commission also found that management and safety issues inside NASA had contributed to the accident.

NASA's quality control staff had decreased by 70 percent since Alan Shepard had walked on the moon in 1971. NASA was under pressure to speed up the launch schedule. The nation's reliance on the shuttle as its principal space launch vehicle created enormous pressure on NASA to increase the flight rate. Technicians worked as many as eighty hours a week, some for two months straight without a day off, trying to meet the launch schedule for that year.[9] "As the flight rate increased, the . . . safety, reliability, and quality assurance work force was decreasing, which adversely affected mission safety," the commission report said.[10] The cause of the accident was due to cold weather, poor human judgment, and mechanical failure of a joint seal in the right solid rocket booster. This tragic accident had a profound effect on future space shuttle launches, at NASA.

From this tragedy came some valuable lessons. However, there would be no more shuttle flights until NASA was sure this would not happen again.

Chapter 5

AFTERMATH

The space shuttle was grounded for thirty-two months after the *Challenger* accident. The largest program of space exploration in history would be put on hold until the shuttle was safe to fly.

▶ Lessons Learned

President Reagan asked NASA to reevaluate the shuttle's place in the space program. As a result, NASA created new goals for shuttle flights. The shuttle's primary mission

△ Senator John Glenn flew as a civilian aboard the space shuttle Discovery in 1998. This was allowed only because Glenn was a former NASA astronaut.

would be to carry the people and supplies needed to build a space station. "Rocket technology is risky," said Sally Ride. "Those risks are something that every astronaut has to internally come to grips with and be willing to accept."[1] NASA changed the policy of civilians flying on the shuttle. Only trained, professional astronauts would fly shuttle missions. Previous civilian crew members included members of Congress and even a prince from Saudi Arabia. There would be no teachers or politicians in space for many years. Senator John Glenn's flight in 1998 was an exception. He had been a trained astronaut.

The Rogers Commission recommended changes to the space shuttle. The most important change was the redesign of the solid rocket booster joints. The engineers redesigned the O-rings, the O-ring seals, and the joints between the booster sections. First, they replaced the putty with an adhesive that made a tighter seal during launch. They added a third O-ring seal, in case the gases reached the adhesive seal. The engineers did not think this would happen, but they were being cautious. They installed temperature sensors and heaters inside the joints. The heaters would keep the temperature of the O-rings at 75°F (23.9°C) at launch. They performed many tests, and the new design performed perfectly during these tests.[2]

The commission called for a new system to manage the shuttle program. NASA would have to establish a flight schedule that did not create safety issues. They also called for better safety and quality control programs. This was to make sure that all materials and procedures were safe.

▶ Keeping Their Memory Alive

To remember the *Challenger* crew, the families of the crew members created the *Challenger* Center for Space Science

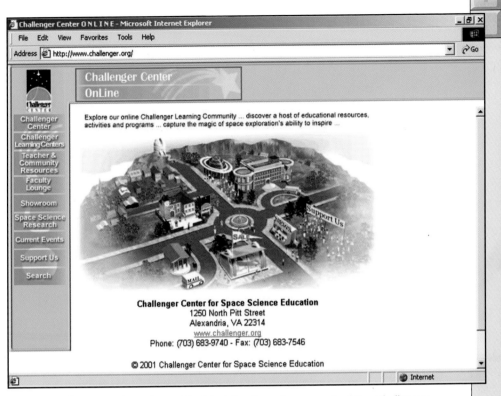

▲ Located in Alexandria, Virginia, the primary goal of the Challenger Center for Space Science Education is to use young people's enthusiasm about space to get them interested in space exploration. The center was founded on April 24, 1986.

Education. There are fifty-two sites located in thirty-one states and Washington, D.C. There are two in Canada and one in the United Kingdom. Their goal is to encourage young people to become interested in science and space travel.

Each center has two rooms. One is a mock-up of the Mission Control room. The other is a space lab. The students role-play as astronauts, mission controllers, and scientists. They solve problems that they may encounter on a real mission. Each student is assigned to one of the

eight teams on the crew. Halfway through the mission, the students switch places so everyone has an opportunity to experience both Mission Control and the space lab.[3]

NASA created the Astronaut Memorial at the Kennedy Space Center. It honors astronauts who have lost their lives in space exploration. The *Challenger* astronauts' names are carved on the black granite surface. The Space Shuttle *Challenger* Memorial in Arlington National Cemetery, near the Tomb of the Unknown Soldier, shows the faces of all seven crew members.

▶ He Never Came Back

The families of the astronauts sued the government and the Morton Thiokol company. Unknown sums were paid to each family. Jane Smith said, "No one in big business should be allowed to make a faulty product and profit from it." Life goes on, and the families have moved on, too. Steven McAuliffe went back to work as a lawyer raising his two children. Cheryl Moore McNair works for a foundation for teenage mothers. Marcia Jarvis clears hiking trails near her home in California. Jane Smith works with her favorite charity, the Virginia Beach Society for the Prevention of Cruelty to Animals. Her dogs, she says, helped her through mourning. She still missed Mike Smith every day: "I waited, and he never came back."[4] She has since remarried.

The debris from *Challenger* was taken to an abandoned launch complex. It was sealed in two eighty-foot-deep missile silos. Debris has washed ashore every so often in the years since the explosion. In December 1996, two pieces of *Challenger* washed up on a beach near the Kennedy Space Center. The pieces were put in the silo where the rest of the shuttle is buried.

Rebirth of the Shuttle Program

On September 29, 1988, *Discovery* launched into the warm, blue Florida sky. The launch was perfect. The O-rings did their job. NASA had learned much from the *Challenger* tragedy. Mission Commander Frederick H. Hauck said, "Today, up here where the blue sky turns to black, we can say at long last, to Dick, Mike, Judy, to Ron and El, and to Christa and to Greg . . . dear friends, we have resumed the journey that we promised to continue for you; . . . your spirit and your dream are still alive in our hearts."[5]

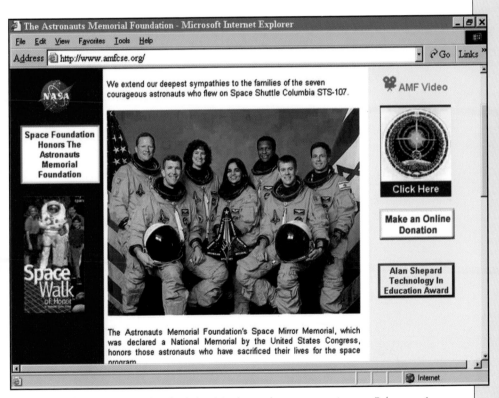

The Astronauts Memorial Foundation - Microsoft Internet Explorer

File   Edit   View   Favorites   Tools   Help

Address http://www.amfcse.org/   Go   Links

We extend our deepest sympathies to the families of the seven courageous astronauts who flew on Space Shuttle Columbia STS-107.

NASA

AMF Video

Space Foundation Honors The Astronauts Memorial Foundation

Click Here

Make an Online Donation

Alan Shepard Technology In Education Award

Space Walk of Honor

The Astronauts Memorial Foundation's Space Mirror Memorial, which was declared a National Memorial by the United States Congress, honors those astronauts who have sacrificed their lives for the space program.

Internet

△ *The space shuttle* Columbia *burned up on reentry on February 1, 2003. This tragedy was a reminder to everyone that space exploration has always been dangerous.*

Safety Record

By October 2002, eighty-six shuttle missions had been launched safely since *Challenger*.[6] The attitude of "hurry up and launch" is gone. In June 2002, NASA discovered a small crack within the fuel lines on *Atlantis*. Instead of launching the next flight, NASA inspected all the shuttles. This meant the expensive removal of the shuttle's main engines. There were similar cracks in all the shuttles. NASA grounded all flights until October. The shuttle did not fly until NASA discovered what caused the cracks and how to prevent them in the future.

Tragedy, though, would strike again. On February 1, 2003, the Space Shuttle *Columbia* exploded as it reentered Earth's atmosphere over the state of Texas. In this case, a piece of insulating foam fell off one of the gas tanks and damaged the left wing of the ship during takeoff. The wing was unable to withstand the heat on reentry, and the entire ship exploded. Seven astronauts were killed.

Educator in Space

At the time of the accident, President Reagan was hopeful. "There will be more shuttle flights," he said, "and more shuttle crews and, yes, more volunteers, more civilians, more teachers in space."[7] NASA, however, said there would be no more civilians on shuttle flights. Still, they left open the possibility for a future Teacher in Space Program. It said, "When NASA determines a flight opportunity is available for a spaceflight participant, first priority will be given to a 'Teacher in Space'. . . ."[8]

Barbara Morgan served as Christa McAuliffe's backup on the *Challenger* mission. She trained with McAuliffe and the *Challenger* crew. She taught reading and math.

△ *Christa McAuliffe (left) is shown here training with her backup, Barbara Morgan (right). Morgan still has hopes of making a space flight.*

When *Challenger* exploded, the Teacher in Space Program ended. Barbara Morgan never gave up her dream of going into space. She returned to her teaching career, but she continued to work with NASA to finish what Christa McAuliffe set out to accomplish. Each year she took her flight physical. She was waiting for the day that NASA would restart the program.

NASA selected Morgan as its first educator mission specialist, and in April 2002, NASA Administrator Sean

O'Keefe said: "The time has come for NASA to complete the mission—to send an educator to space to inspire and teach our young people, . . . We will make Barbara's (Morgan) flight the first in a series of missions in the new Educator in Space program."[9]

Morgan works in the Mission Control Center as the communicator with shuttle crews. She was scheduled to fly after completion of the core elements of the International Space Station, in 2004. However, on February 1, 2003, the explosion of the space shuttle *Columbia* changed those plans. The remaining three space shuttles were grounded indefinitely until investigators could determine the cause of the accident. Then they would have to put procedures in place so that an explosion like that would not likely happen again. Only the Russian *Soyuz* and *Progress* rockets were left to resupply the International Space Station. "What happened (with *Challenger*) was horrible," said Morgan, "and you can't ever erase that. But our job as teachers is to help kids reach their potential. *Challenger* reminds us that we should never quit reaching for the stars."[10]

Chapter 1. The Final Voyage

1. Robert T. Hohler, *I Touch the Future. . . : The Story of Christa McAuliffe* (New York: Random House, 1986), p. 49.

2. Author witness to launch of shuttle *Columbia*, April 4, 1981.

3. Steve Garber, curator, "Transcript of the *Challenger* Crew Comments From the Operational Recorder," *National Aeronautics and Space Administration,* February 3, 2003, <http://www.hq.nasa .gov/office/pao/History/transcript.html> (October 30, 2002).

4. David Shayler, *Shuttle Challenger* (New York: Prentice Hall Press), 1987, p. 49.

Chapter 2. Launch Background

1. Robert T. Hohler, *I Touch the Future. . . : The Story of Christa McAuliffe* (New York: Random House, 1986), p. 248.

2. Jay Barbree, "Chapter 1: A Chill at the Cape," MSNBC News, 2003, <http://www.msnbc.com/news/510544.asp> (October 30, 2002).

3. Richard Lewis, *Challenger: The Final Voyage* (New York: Columbia University Press, 1988), p. 131.

4. Barbree, "A Chill at the Cape."

5. Ed Magnuson, "The Slipped the Surly Bonds of Earth to Touch the Face of God," *Time*, February 10, 1986, p. 26.

6. Kay Grinter, curator, "Space Shuttle TAL Sites," *John F. Kennedy Space Center,* May 15, 2001, <http://www-pao.ksc.nasa .gov/kscpao/nasafact/tal.htm#top> (October 30, 2002).

7. Magnuson, p. 26.

8. Lewis, p. 3.

9. Tommy W. Holloway, "Mission Planning and Operation Team Report," *Report of the Presidential Commission on the Space Shuttle Challenger Accident,* May 1986, <http://history .nasa.gov/rogersrep/v2appj.htm> (October 30, 2002).

10. David Shayler, *Shuttle Challenger* (New York: Prentice Hall Press, 1987), p. 49.

11. Joseph P. Kerwin, "Letter to Admiral Richard H. Truly," *National Aeronautics and Space Administration, July 28, 1986,* <http://www.hq.nasa.gov/office/pao/History/kerwin.html> (October 30, 2002)

12. Magnuson, p. 25.

13. Claudia Glenn Dowling, "Ten Years Ago, Seven Brave Americans Died as They Reached for the Stars," *Life,* February 1996, p. 39.

14. Lewis, p. 22.

15. Claudia Glenn Dowling, "From the February 1996 issue of Life," *The Mission Continues,* n.d., <http://www.life.com/Life/space/challenger/challenger04.html> (October 30, 2002).

16. Malcolm McConnell, *Challenger: A Major Malfunction* (Garden City, N.Y.: Doubleday & Company, Inc., 1987), p. 247.

17. Ronald Reagan, "The White House, January 28, 1986," *Reagan's Remarks,* <http://www.chron.com/content/interactive/special/challenger/docs/reagan.html> (October 30, 2002).

18. Kerwin, "Letter to Admiral Richard H. Truly."

19. Ibid.

20. Ibid.

Chapter 3. The Seven Heroes

1. Paul Gray, "Seven Who Flew for All of Us," *Time,* February 10, 1986, p. 33.

2. Ibid.

3. Ibid., p. 34.

4. Ibid., p. 35.

5. Robert T. Hohler, *I Touch the Future. . . : The Story of Christa McAuliffe* (New York: Random House, 1986), p. 5.

6. Ibid.

7. Ibid., p. 55.

8. Ibid., p. 97.

9. Ibid., p. 64.

10. Richard Lewis, *Challenger: The Final Voyage* (New York: Columbia University Press, 1988), p. 1.

11. Hohler, p. 170.

12. Ibid., p. 150.

13. Ronald Reagan, "A President's Eulogy," *1st Anniversary, January 31, 1986,* <http://www.chron.com/content/interactive/special/challenger/docs/eulogy.html> (October 30, 2002).

Chapter 4. Anatomy of the Accident

1. Cliff Lethbridge, "The *Challenger* Legacy," *Spaceline,* 2000, <http://www.spaceline.org/challenger.html#3> (October 30, 2002).

2. Tommy W. Holloway, "Mission Planning and Operation Team Report," *Report of the Presidential Commission on the Space Shuttle Challenger Accident, May 1986,* <http://history.nasa.gov/rogersrep/v1ch3.htm> (October 30, 2002).

3. Richard Lewis, *Challenger: The Final Voyage* (New York: Columbia University Press, 1988), p. 63.

4. Holloway, "Mission Planning and Operation Team Report."

5. Lewis, p. 76.

6. Ibid.

7. Ibid., p. 126.

8. Wayne Biddle, "What Destroyed *Challenger?*" *Discover,* April 1986, p. 46.

9. Robert T. Hohler, *I Touch the Future. . . : The Story of Christa McAuliffe* (New York: Random House, 1986), p. 235.

10. Holloway, "Mission Planning and Operation Team Report."

Chapter 5. Aftermath

1. Laura S. Woodmansee, *Women Astronauts* (Ontario, Canada: Apogee Books, 2002), p. 44.

2. "The *Challenger* Accident: An Analysis of the Mechanical and Administrative Causes of the Accident and the Redesign Process that Followed," Mechanical Redesign, n.d., <http://www.me.utexas.edu/~uer/challenger/chall4.html#oringerosion> (October 30, 2002).

3. "*Challenger* Learning Centers," *Challenger Center for Space Science Education,* 2003, <http://www.challenger.org/clc/clc_tell_set.htm> (October 30, 2002).

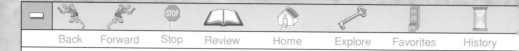

4. Claudia Glenn Dowling, "From the February 1996 issue of Life," *The Mission Continues,* n.d., <http://www.life.com/Life/space/challenger/challenger05.html> (October 30, 2002).

5. "MCC Status Reports," Spacelink, 1988, <http://spacelink.nasa.gov/NASA.Projects/Human.Exploration .and.Development.of.Space/Human.Space.Flight/Shuttle/ Shuttle.Missions/Flight.026.STS-26/MCC.Status.Reports> (October 30, 2002).

6. Jim Dumoulin, "NASA Space Shuttle Launches," *Space Shuttle Launches,* February 1, 2003, <http://science.ksc.nasa .gov/shuttle/missions/> (October 30, 2002).

7. Dowling, "From the February 1996 issue of *Life.*"

8. "Aeronautics and Space," *Code of Federal Regulations,* January 1, 2003, <http://a257.g.akamaitech.net/7/257/2422/ 14mar20010800/edocket.acces.../14cfr1214.303.htm) (September 17, 2003).

9. Bob Jacobs, "Administrator Unveils Future NASA Vision and a Renewed Journey of Learning," *NASA,* <ftp://ftp.hq .nasa.gov/pub/pao/pressrel/2002/02-066.txt> (October 30, 2002).

10. Dowling, "From the February 1996 issue of *Life.*"

Further Reading

Biel, Timothy Levi. *The Challenger.* San Diego, Calif.: Lucent Books, 1990.

Bond, Peter. *Guide to Space.* New York: Dorling Kindersley, Inc., 1999.

Bredeson, Carmen. *The Challenger Disaster—Tragic Spaceflight.* Berkeley Heights, N.J.: Enslow Publishers, Inc., 1999.

Bricker, Susan D. *Challenger.* Buena Park, Calif.: Aresian Press, 1999.

Chippendale, Lisa. *Apollo One/Challenger.* Broomall, Pa.: Chelsea House Publishers, 2000.

Corrigan, Grace G. *A Journal for Christa.* Lincoln and London: University of Nebraska Press, 1993.

Gold, Susan D. *To Space and Back: The Story of the Shuttle.* Parsippany, N.J.: Silver Burdett Press, 1992.

Lieurance, Suzanne. *The Space Shuttle Challenger Disaster in American History.* Berkeley Heights, N.J.: Enslow Publishers, Inc., 2001.

McNeese, Tim. *The Challenger Disaster.* Danbury, Conn.: Scholastic Library Publishing, 2003.

Naden, Corinne J., and Rose Blue. *Christa McAuliffe: Teacher in Space.* Brookfield, Conn.: Millbrook Press, Inc., 1991.

Staff. *The Challenger Disaster.* Boston: Houghton Mifflin Company, 1992.

Stott, Carole. *Space Exploration.* New York: Alfred A. Knopf, 1997.

Index